Problem Solving,
Reasoning and Numeracy
in the
Early Years Foundation Stage

by
Dr Hannah Mortimer

A QEd Publication

Published in 2003
Revised in 2008

© Hannah Mortimer

ISBN 978 1 898873 55 6

British Library Cataloguing
A catalogue record for this book is available from the British Library.

Published by QEd Publications, 39 Weeping Cross, Stafford ST17 0DG
Tel: 01785 620364
Fax: 01785 607797
Website: www.qed.uk.com
Email: orders@qed.uk.com

Printed by Gutenberg Press Ltd, Malta.

Contents

Introduction

Who this book is for

This book will be useful for early years educators working in all kinds of Early Years Foundation Stage (EYFS) settings: childminders, pre-schools, private nurseries, day nurseries and schools. It will also be helpful for individuals training on NVQ or pre-school diploma courses and of interest to childminders, parents and carers of children in their early years. In other words, it will be of interest to all those who live or work with children of five or under and who wish to support their early development in problem solving, reasoning and numeracy. It has been written so that it is equally relevant to those living and working with children and babies under three as for those working in registered settings for three and four-year-olds.

About this book

In the first chapter, we consider the first year or so of life and discover how even babies are learning problem solving concepts as they try to make sense of their world. Chapter Two takes this further and considers the stage of exploring and 'finding' out that toddlers and most one-year-olds have reached. Chapter Three considers the typical problem solving, reasoning and numeracy of a two-year-old and in Chapter Four we explore the understanding of quantity and number in the typical three to four-year-old in a setting. Chapter Four also reminds us of the EYFS framework for three to four-year-olds and the Early Learning Goals.

How can early years workers work and play alongside children to support and encourage their learning? We now know that the best approaches to help young children learn are a combination of exploration through play and guided teaching and support. But what might this 'look like' in early problem solving, reasoning and numeracy?

The age ranges are only a rough guide and it will make most sense to look at the developmental stage that the children in your care have reached. Even if you live or work with three to five-year-olds, you should find that a knowledge and understanding of how skills develop will help you teach and encourage each child more effectively, since you will have grasped 'where they are coming from' in their learning. This also makes it easier for you to plan for any individual or special needs. Chapter Five considers children who have special educational needs and how you can plan, along with parents and carers, how to support their early problem solving, reasoning and numeracy.

The whole book is written in simple terms so that it can be kept as concrete and practical as possible for early years workers, parents and carers at all stages of experience. To make it easier to read, alternating sections have been written using 'he' or 'she'. There are some useful references and suggestions for further reading at the back.

Chapter One

Baby problem solving

Earliest stages

In the first year of his life the new baby is learning how to make sense of his world. With sounds, shapes, movements, colours and feelings all around, how can he begin to make predictions about what will happen next and whether sensations herald 'good news' or 'bad news'? At first, these are a buzzing confusion of sensations and the new baby does not have any sense of how they are linked together or even that he is a little person in his own right. At the same time, he has been born almost pre-programmed to learn and will actively be seeking out sounds, sights and touch as the weeks go by. He begins to learn that the sound of steps on the stairs means that his carer is nearby and he turns to look or he cries louder. He begins to learn that the fist waving in front of his eyes belongs to him and he can move it at will. He begins to learn that he can knock his mobile and it makes a sound which he can then repeat. He also begins to learn that if a toy disappears momentarily from view it still exists to be found again.

This ability to learn that toys and people continue to exist even when he cannot see them is called *object permanence* and is a vital early stage to understanding quantity and number. Though it seems obvious to an older person, it comes as a genuine surprise to a young baby that the same person who disappeared into the next room should reappear again. It is as if he forgets it was ever there, because what he cannot see ceases to exist for him. In simple terms, once he has developed object permanence, the baby is counting *one*. He can either count *one* of a person standing over him, or he cannot and he therefore looks for that person. This is perhaps the first sign of clever baby number work and parents and carers can use 'peep bo' and hiding games to develop early object permanence. You will find a helpful book full of number games for babies and young children listed on page 44.

How early numeracy develops

Babies can develop an interest in numbers from a very early age. Young children learn best through playing and through interactions and games with people and objects around them. Play that is best for development is play that is at just the right developmental level for the child, or even that slightly stretches her. If they can provide the right opportunities, the right materials and be supportive and encouraging, parents and carers can help their young children to become successful learners. One of the starting points in problem solving, reasoning and numeracy is to help children develop an interest in numbers, learn to count by rote and develop one-to-one correspondence using anticipation, number rhymes and counting aloud. The activities adults do with children do not necessarily have to contain numbers and counting – there are many early stages to number which can be built on usefully before moving on to counting, as this book explains.

How do babies begin to become interested in number shapes and written numbers? Because growing babies are so interested in sounds and shapes, it is possible to introduce colourful number shapes early on for her to look at. Numbers are interesting to look at and have interesting edges and contours. Parents and carers can also use number rhymes in their songs from the earliest age so that the rhythm of the words becomes familiar and is linked with enjoyment and playing. Number shapes can be used as part of the nursery or play area – number mobiles which sparkle and turn, numbers on wall charts and posters, early picture books with simple numbers and sets of objects to count. Even before a baby is ready to do this herself, adults can be counting and playing with numbers, making them an enjoyable experience.

Early counting

Young babies will probably have become familiar with hearing adults count long before they have a go themselves. They have to learn how to make speech sounds and to master early words before they can say the numbers back. However, the rhyme and rhythm of counting can be introduced from an early age by building this into daily activities, songs and rhymes. The first counting will probably come as part of a well-rehearsed phrase which the baby associates with pleasure. This might be a playful 'one, two, three …' leading into a swing or a cuddle. If this is done often enough, the baby might echo the vowel sounds 'u – oo – ee' (for 'one – two – three') even before his words are clear. Later he might add a final number 'eeeee!' to a count of 'one – two ...'.

Seeing shapes

The ability to see the difference between shapes and to respond differently to them (known as *discrimination*) again develops very early on. It is a basic skill which all animals need to have in order to identify sources of food, danger and comfort. In fact, studies on octopuses have shown that they are well able to discriminate between a circle or a square if their food is always hidden behind one. In the same way, new babies soon become able to identify familiar adults from their general shape and movement, their facial features, their smell and their voice. Carers will notice her move her body more as she sees them approach, or perhaps *still* to the sound of their voices.

Young babies seem to arrive pre-programmed to take an interest in certain patterns of light and shade around them. For example, they are predisposed to look at and study faces that come within their focus. After a few months, a baby might be observed staring intently at her own hands and fingers as if she has recognised for the first time that these waving objects belong to her. She will quickly learn to recognise the pattern that her fingers make and link these to the feelings of touch she receives from them and the movements she can make with them – this is all part of a clever eye-hand co-ordination. After a few months, she will begin to take an interest in objects and toys around her as well as faces. She will begin to make swiping movements with her arms and occasionally come into contact with these. From this point, she begins to make the links between seeing and reaching out towards something.

Number and shape spotting

We have seen that the ability to see the difference between shapes and to respond differently to them (known as *discrimination*) develops very early on. If a baby is to be able to recognise number shapes and discriminate these from letters and other shapes, then he will first need to develop his looking skills and his ability to perceive different shapes and rotations and lines. So the experiences he has that help to develop *shape* recognition will also be helping his ability to spot and 'read' written *numbers* later on.

As he plays, he is learning that he can actively move his hands or feet in order to touch or influence things around him. Through these rather random movements come purpose and intention. Through his early explorations comes the dawning that things in the world are *different* or *the same*. This understanding of *same* and *different* leads on to the baby's first understanding of simple concepts and categories such as shape, quantity and colour.

Understanding size and space

It takes a while for a baby to develop the stereoscopic vision to be able to tell different sizes and distances apart – in other words, a small ball close up will look the same to her as a large ball further away. As she begins to handle different sizes of objects, she will begin to develop a better understanding of this. At first, she will not realise that a small car seen from close up is a different size from a large car seen from across a street. It is only by playing and interacting with different-sized objects and experimenting with moving around herself that she will make links between distances, depths and sizes. In other words, she will develop *stereoscopic vision*, allowing her two eyes to work together and link this to her knowledge of how big things are in order to judge how far away they are.

Understanding of size again develops naturally as a baby becomes more experienced in the objects around her. Cot covers and clothing all have interesting feels and textures and she will soon learn that she can pull and tug these around to cover or uncover different parts of herself. As she begins to play at emptying or filling containers she will begin to grasp that certain things can be fitted inside others but not the other way round. In other words, different sizes will begin to become *significant* to her play.

Sequences of actions

The first sequence that a baby will learn about is that one thing generally leads to another. This is also called *linking cause with effect*. This ability can be encouraged through play which helps the child to make these connections. Counting and numbers all follow given sequences and can develop out of his early attempts to carry out a simple sequence of actions. Getting dressed and undressed also provide natural occasions for building up familiar sequences and routines. He will learn from his daily routines that one time of day leads on to another and this is one of the reasons why having a fairly predictable routine helps him to feel confident and to learn.

Sequences of time

Understanding sequences is an important part of learning about numbers. One of the first sequences that a baby will understand is the sequence of *time* and this will come naturally as you take her through predictable daily *routines*. New babies follow their own routines rather than an adult's. They wake and sleep according to the signals from their own bodies – when they feel tired, when they are uncomfortable, when they are hungry, when they are full. Each baby has been born with the instinct to cry when she needs something and this is her way of communicating with the adults around her.

Experts used to believe that we should impose routines on babies right from the early days, but we now know that we should read the messages a new baby is giving us and respond to them on demand. This is all part of forming the warm relationships between babies and their carers which will lead to more settled and confident babies. When the child is a few months older, she will be able to choose whether she wakes or sleeps to a certain extent and routines become a natural and important part of family or nursery life. Children's confidence grows from having a warm and secure relationship with the adults in their company. We now know that some of the best ways of forming this relationship are for carers to tune in to what their baby is trying to tell them, and to share pleasure and fun together.

Supporting their learning

- Use gentle routines and calmness to establish confidence and try not to overwhelm a young baby with stimulation when he is still at the point of making sense of it all. Babies learn best when they are neither too aroused nor too sleepy.

- Use a similar voice as you approach to help him link the sound of your voice with your face and your actions. Even tiny babies are fascinated by faces, so look at him and talk as you feed him. This will help him make links between his senses and begin to see the world as a predictable place.

- 'Peep-bo' and 'hide and seek' games are great fun and encourage object permanence in older babies.

- Encourage older babies to search for items that they have dropped, to look down as items fall from the highchair or to find something you have hidden close by.

- Select toys and playthings that help the child to find out about shapes, sizes and numbers in the world around and talk to him about simple patterns and designs.

- Use a variety of safe, brightly coloured baby toys of different shapes and textures for him to look at and explore with his hands and mouth.

- Introduce the words for different shapes early on, even if he cannot yet understand these – a *round* bowl, a *square* brick, etc.

- Provide him with brightly coloured three-dimensional shapes to handle and explore which are safe to put in the mouth – cubes, boxes, balls, cylinders, etc.

- Encourage him to play with shape posting and shape matching games as soon as he is interested.

- Use a number mobile, wall chart or poster to make numbers familiar and fun – you can talk about numbers even before he is old enough to understand everything you say.

- Even when he is very young, say *up* and *down* as you lift him and lay him down again.

- Begin to provide him with simple containers and boxes for emptying and filling when he is a few months old. Let him have his own safe cupboard to empty, and put safety catches on the others.

- Build up familiar routines and rituals throughout the day – a certain pattern to each day, a certain bedtime routine for settling him at night.

- Ask questions such as 'Where's Mummy?' just as Mummy is about to appear round the corner.

- Repeat sounds that you make so that your baby can begin to hear similar patterns.

- Use a few familiar toys and cuddlies to help him understand what *sameness* is.

Chapter Two

Toddlerhood and exploration

Interesting shapes

Most toddlers and one-year-olds will enjoy handling objects and toys and will take a delight in posting things in and emptying them out of containers (or indeed any openings they can find). An 18-month-old will probably be able to match a large circle to a large space on a shape board and a small circle to a small space, using mostly a trial-and-error approach. By about 21 months, she will be posting round pegs into round holes and taking an interest in posting box games. Around her second birthday, she will probably be able to match a circle, a square and a triangle to their correct places on a shape form-board – typically she will manage the circle first, then the square and later the triangle.

One-year-olds and toddlers will enjoy handling numbers and can play with the shapes of a number form-board long before they are old enough to fit the pieces into place.

Most toddlers will find it easier to look at written numbers and name them if they have played with them and shown a genuine interest in them first. Adults can help young children develop confidence in numbers by avoiding direct questioning ('How many are there?' or 'What's this number?') and talking about number naturally instead, emphasising key words ('I wonder *how many* – shall we *count* them together?' or 'Oh look! Can you see the number *one*? Bryony is *one* as well!').

Making simple comparisons

The earliest stage of making comparisons will emerge out of the baby's ability to see, touch and explore his world. We have already discovered that, long before he has the language or understanding to say that things are the *same* or *different*, he will explore touching, swiping, feeling and mouthing anything that his hands come into contact with. He is already becoming a little scientist, working out what he must do to move his body in order to explore his surroundings – how to swipe his arms to jiggle the mobile or how to reach and grasp to secure the rattle. This early stage has already laid the foundations for his understanding of *cause and effect*.

It is only after he has had chances to link together what he sees, touches and feels that he can then begin to make sense of which things in his world go together into sets or *concepts*. Now he is ready to begin sorting and matching. At first, this comes naturally and all that is needed is plenty of opportunity to explore with an interested adult close by to provide the words and commentary to help him learn. Using comparison words such as 'same' and 'different' are an important part of early number development and are best taught by linking words to actions when the child is playing freely.

More or less – understanding change

As part of their mathematical development, children have to develop their understanding of quantity and respond to words such as more, less, lots and all gone. Young children learn best from familiar everyday situations so meal-times provide a wealth of opportunity for handling quantity and for seeing how amounts change as you eat up or ask for more.

There is a wonderful stage round the first birthday when children suddenly begin to *gather* objects. Most of them will delight in picking up toys and collecting them together in containers, spending happy times emptying and filling, over and over again. At this stage, the child begins to combine objects together in her play, banging them together, stacking one on top of another, lining them up. It suddenly becomes clear that she has the idea that certain objects can be the *same* and can be used or collected together in some way. This stage has to come before she can begin to understand sets and quantities. You can tell from her play that she is gathering *more* and knows when she has *less*. The fact that she is playing with sets of objects means that she is gaining important experiences about how quantities change as she manipulates and handles them.

Lots and lots – understanding quantity

Before any child starts to count how many, he will probably refer to things as *lots*. This is his first counting, since he recognises when he has just one or two and when he has plenty. It is amusing to hear older children counting 'one, two, three, lots'. From his early games with sets of objects and quantity of food, he will begin to make judgements about quantity based on how things look – and this visual judgement will become most important when he later learns to count reliably. So understanding *lots* is a clever number stage that he will pass through.

Naming numbers

Before a child can make the link between written numbers (e.g. '2') and *how many* these represent (such as 'two spoons'), she will have to develop an understanding of sets – that is, different quantities of objects. Adults can help by planning games and activities which need not have any written numbers at the early stages but are played to help the developing toddler make links in her thinking between different quantities and sets – *one* candle on a cake or *two* biscuits on a plate. This will help her to grasp how to use numbers and how they relate to different amounts of things. You will find whole series of games for developing early number skills and which relate to the developmental ideas in this present booklet listed on page 44.

Position and direction

Through their everyday activities, young children can be encouraged to follow directions, understand size and space, anticipate and copy action sequences, and respond to simple position and time words such as *up*, *down*, *before* and *after*. These are important aspects of mathematical development. A baby's first experiences of position words such as *up* and *down* will occur naturally as he is lifted up and placed down throughout the day. From an early age, he will begin to anticipate what is going to happen next when he is greeted in the morning, wriggling into position or raising his arms up to be lifted. One of his first words is quite likely to be *up* or *down* as he is lifted or played with, since he knows that these words go hand in hand with a definite action or intention.

When he is about one year old, he will delight in emptying and filling containers and will build up an understanding of *in* and *out* even before he has the language to understand what the words mean. At first, toys that fall out of his sight will be gone for ever as far as he is concerned, but once he understands the conservation of quantity – in other words that things continue to exist even when you cannot see them – he will begin to look *underneath, in, behind*. The understanding of direction words such as *come, go, forwards* and *backwards* tends to come a little later when he has learned how to move around, how to change direction as he walks or trots and also when he begins to see other points of view – around two years of age.

Building on routines

As the child grows a little older and reaches 'toddlerdom', she will appreciate that life has certain patterns and routines to it and that experiences and objects in the world can be *same* or *different*. Toddlers can sometimes negotiate and push boundaries to their limits if there is no routine or pattern to the day. Between one and two, she will be making links between what she does and the effect it has on others. This is where routines can really help – if she learns that shouting loud enough always brings a parent or carer back after bedtime, it could develop into a game of its own. Routines help children understand the passage of time. They also help the child learn that one thing inevitably leads to another, to begin to *anticipate* what will happen next and help the child feel secure and *contained* by the adults around.

Supporting their learning

- Play with sets of objects – cars, teddies, bricks, spoons, plastic cups, currants, seedless grapes ... the choice is endless. Make sure the non-food items cannot be swallowed.

- Provide containers, bowls, pans for him to put things in and take them out again.

- Use meal-times as a chance to play with quantities and expect him to touch and play with his food in the early stages – it is all part of learning and feeling relaxed about feeding. Be prepared for mess with a plastic sheet on the floor and plenty of bibs and wipes.

- You can introduce the words *more* and *all gone* regularly as you feed him.

- Sand and water are useful starting points for play because they change in quantity as you handle them.

- Introduce the word *lots* in your everyday conversations and at meal-times.

- Use snack-times to develop early counting – counting out the biscuits, pieces of fruit, pieces of sausage, chips … *you* can start counting regularly long before your child does and make spoken numbers an enjoyable part of your daily meal-times.

- Make use of natural opportunities to spot numbers such as on sticker birthday badges and door numbers. Point these out to your child and look out for the number that is the same as his age.

- Look out for toys that have numbers as part of them – there are many form-boards, puzzles and early number toys available now which you can play with long before your child can understand *maths*.

- Provide chances for early counting by providing sets made up of lots of the same thing – e.g. cotton reels, bricks, shoes, etc.

- Count out the cups for tea or the videos to go in the cupboard and point to the written number on a wall frieze, mobile or poster.

- Provide plenty of toys and playthings for putting in and emptying out again. Talk to him as he plays, emphasising the position words: '*In* they go! *Out* they come!'

- Play a game between two of you when he is learning to walk, sending him first to one and then to the other: '*Away* you go! *Back* you come!'

- Even toddlers will enjoy simple games in which they join in with a 'yes' or a 'no' when you ask if two things are the *same*.

- Provide a running commentary yourself as your child plays and explores ('they are both blue!') and look for natural opportunities to use words such as *same* and *different*. Keep your language very simple, emphasising the key words.

- Build in little rituals to your daily life – a bath-time song; settling the teddies into bed; an order for putting on coats, shoes and hats when you go out; a clunk-click of the seat belt in the car; a story or song at the end of a play session, etc.

- Use photographs to talk about what happened in the past and what will happen in the future (for instance going on holiday or going on an outing).

- Count naturally through the day – 'one sock on, two socks on', 'one step, two steps'.

- Introduce number rhymes and chants from an early age so that children become familiar with the rhythm and sound of the counting words.

Chapter Three

The in-betweens: under threes

Shapes and symbols

At the age of about two, children begin to enjoy exploring shapes and playing with all kinds of simple shape boards and early jigsaws. They will enjoy experimenting with and placing different-sized nesting toys inside of each other, or stacking them to make a tower. They will point to the *big* one or the *little* one if you ask and will begin to use these words spontaneously in their play. Written numbers are just one kind of shape which have come to be used regularly by us as *symbols* – something that represents a concept such as a *quantity*. Even before three years old, children will be able to spot and take an interest in numbers around them, and begin to realise that these are different from letters and words. They will be able to spot familiar numbers on road signs and on packaging and take a pride in 'reading' these out loud – 'Look! There's a 3!' By two to three years old, they are beginning to link number symbols with words and may show a delight in the birthday cards and badges, pointing out the *two* or the *three*. As soon as a child begins to recognise certain numbers, e.g. *1, 2* or *3*, it is helpful for carers and children to spend time together looking out for these numbers in packaging, house numbers and everyday situations.

One-to-one

The ability to link one counting number with one object is called developing *one-to-one correspondence*. At first, a child learns to count *by rote*. That means that she can remember a string of numbers and recite them *one, two, three, four, five*. However, if you place five bricks in front of her, she is most likely to touch the first brick and finish chanting 'one, two, three, four, five' long before she touches the last brick. She has not yet learned to touch one and count one and this is a normal step in development. When you think about it, it is still very clever that she knows that touching and counting can go together. In other words, she has grasped the idea that *quantity* can be counted and numbered. In time, she will learn to count the bricks methodically, saying one number for each brick touched. She will then have developed an understanding of *one-to-one correspondence*. Typically, children count by rote to about ten before they begin to count out objects to four or five, so it is a skill that slightly follows the ability to count by rote.

Patterns around us

We are surrounded by patterns all around us – a pattern is a repeated shape, line or arrangement which can either be regular (like the pattern of bricks in a wall, the railings in a fence, the tiles on a floor, the cans on a supermarket shelf or the repeated pattern of wallpaper) or random (like crazy paving, pebbles on the beach or flowers in a meadow). We can help young children to become aware of patterns in our environment by pointing them out and also by providing items for children to form their own arrangements and patterns. This is all part of early mathematics and involves the important skills of visual discrimination, understanding how spaces and shapes can relate to each other and making predictions. Encourage children to talk about patterns that they see and to guess what comes next. You can start by choosing a very simple sequence – perhaps lining up a teddy, a cat, a teddy and a car – can the child continue the pattern all by himself? In the early years, it is important to keep sequences and patterns really simple since too much information can overwhelm and confuse them.

Recognising simple sets

Learning that things around can be the *same* or *different* helps the child see that certain objects go together into sets and can be sorted, counted and matched. If a child is going to be able to count things, then he needs to be able to grasp that things around him can be the same or different. In other words, he cannot possibly count out six cups and three saucers unless he can see that cups and saucers are different things in the first place. This ability to count groups of the same thing is called counting *sets* – a *set* is any quantity of the same sort of thing like cars, counters, bricks or teddy bears. In sets, objects belong together because they have a common property – for example, a round object belongs to a set of round objects because it has the property of being round like all the others. One of the earliest number skills for a child to learn is the ability to make simple comparisons between sets or groups of objects. At first, he will develop this as part of his regular playing and exploring. He might place two blue cars together or pick up two bricks at once. Once he has learned to match like things together, then he will be able to sort (for example, placing all the toy cars in one tub and all the toy people in another), and later identify (handing the yellow one over when asked, 'Which is the *yellow* one?') and later name ('That's a cat!' 'That's red!'). Remembering this sequence – match, sort, identify, name – is a helpful aid when planning activities that are easier or harder depending on the stage the child has reached.

What stages do children go through when they are learning to match? Typically, a child will match *real objects* first (e.g. placing cups together or collecting cars in her hands), then *photographs* to objects (e.g. matching a photo of Grandad to Grandad himself), then *pictures* to objects (matching a drawing of a dog to the real dog), then *colours* (placing red bricks into a red box), then *sizes* (matching big balls or little balls), then more complex *characteristics* such as *long/short*, *high/low*, *full/empty* and *heavy/light*.

Concept development

We have seen how early mathematical development involves all kinds of skills and activities. These go far beyond simply learning about numbers and how to count. They include exploring shape, colour and size, and making comparisons between things. Children have to be able to distinguish between *same* and *different* if they are to match and sort, to group objects into categories and concepts, to notice and create patterns and sequences and to appreciate how quantity changes. With this understanding comes the ability to begin to form *concepts* and to make links in their thinking – that red, blue and green are all *colours* and that squares, circles and triangles are all *shapes*.

First and last

Another kind of comparison which any child will learn to make is one of *first* and *last*. We call position numbers such as 'first', 'second' and 'third' *ordinal* numbers. Typically, a child will learn to count by rote ('one, two, three') before she will understand or use ordinal numbers. Children can collect early experience of these if the words are introduced into regular daily language: '*Last* sock!' 'You're *first!*' Dressing and undressing times provide plenty of opportunity for talking about the order in which things happen. She will also be able to learn about sequences – how one thing usually leads on to another – which is another vital aspect to learning how to handle words, numbers and language later on. Learning sequences of actions helps a child to understand the passage of time and how events in the world relate together. That is one of the reasons why familiar routines are so helpful.

Writing it down

Children usually tend to start writing numbers at age three to four, but it will take a while before they can form these correctly. Usually they write 1, 2 and 3 before they make an attempt at higher numbers. Before he reaches the stage of being able to copy or remember how to write a number, he will need to learn how to control a crayon or felt-tip pen, how to make straight lines and how to make circular lines. Before he can learn how to write numbers to represent a quantity of something, he will need to make links between what numbers *look* like, what they *feel* like to write and *how many* they represent.

By playing with children from an early age matching, posting, scribbling, holding and manipulating, carers will be teaching all the hand-eye co-ordination skills needed to help them learn to write numbers later on. By adding their own commentary to help the children count and to point out what written numbers 'say', they will also be helping to form links between counting, writing and reading numbers.

Supporting their learning

- Try not to give the impression that there is a right way and a wrong way of playing with numbers and always make the child feel successful.

- Start by introducing numbers 1 to 3 and then build up to 5 when the child is ready. Do not move too quickly – there is time enough to build on these early stages.

- Play games that involve counting by rote before you start counting out objects.

- Count out plates, cups, spoons as you lay them on the table together and count the stairs as you go up and down.

- When she begins to join in with you, leave out alternate words for her to fill in – 'One ... (two) ... three ... (four) ...'.

- Play games that involve give and take: 'Give me *two* cars', 'Here is *one* tractor' and guide the child's finger to touch as she counts. Help your child arrange objects in a line before counting them out, moving from left to right.

- Play games sorting the socks into pairs, sorting the spoons from the forks, finding cups and saucers that go together. Toy tea services in primary colours give good opportunities for matching colours and developing one-to-one correspondence.

- Look for opportunities to introduce the words for opposites and differences – 'Look! That's *full*! Now it's *empty*!' Enjoy emptying and filling games together as you explore how quantities change.

- Start by introducing the words *first* and *last* into your daily conversations in natural situations. Move on to introducing *second* and *third*, perhaps using a natural game such as playing with trucks or doing up buttons.

- Choose toys that involve grading different sizes – size shape boards, stacking rings, stacking beakers, size posting toys.

- Use the words *big* and *small* or *little* in your play together so that they begin to link these words with the appearance of an object.

- Spot written numbers together as you handle shopping or go on journeys.

- Choose toys that involve pattern making – chunky beads or cotton reels to thread, coloured peg or mosaic boards, construction or interlocking toys to be pieced together in different arrangements.

- Look out for repeating patterns as you travel around together – the rails of a fence, the squares on a pavement, the countdown signs on a motorway.

- Use hand prints and finger painting to make your own repeated patterns and use this to make wrapping paper or a wall poster.

- Look for writing and drawing implements that are good for small and chubby hands to hold – chubby crayons, egg-shaped chalks, finger crayons, etc. You can refine her skills onto finer pencils and felt-tips later on as she becomes more controlled.

- Show her how to make straight lines and circular scribbles and to enjoy mark-making. Write numbers in yellow felt-tip for her to copy over – keep these large at first and guide her hand if she will let you.

- Look for chances for her to make links between the number she is writing and actual counting – three ducks in the bath, perhaps, or two plates on the table.

- Provide plenty of small world play such as a Noah's ark, a toy farmyard, a dolls' house, a garage or a train track and talk her through the positions: 'Look! Thomas is *in* the shed!'

- Start asking 'where?' questions when she is older to encourage her to use position words in her talking. Make the most of sand and water play so that she can enjoy filling, pouring, sinking things, burying them, finding them again.

- Provide a variety of shaped paper for drawing and scribbling on. Look out for shape and size matching puzzles and inset-boards.

- Make a visual timetable for your child so that she can see from a sequence of photographs what is going to happen first each day and what happens next – eating breakfast, going to nursery, etc.

- Enjoy action rhymes and games together which will make repeating sequences of actions fun.

- As the child gets older, longer periods will be spent in constructing and building; this is excellent for developing both concentration and mathematical ability.

- When playing number games together, try to enjoy the *process* rather than the *product*. The main aim is for you to enjoy your time together so if a game is not working, simply drop it and try something else.

Chapter Four

Four and five year-olds

In this chapter, we explore problem solving, reasoning and numeracy in the typical three to four-year-old at pre-school, nursery or in reception class. We now know that the best approaches to help young children learn are a combination of exploration through play and guided teaching and support, but what might this 'look like' in practice? There are national guidelines – *The Early Years Foundation Stage: Practice Guidance* (DfES, 2007) and one of the Areas of Learning covered in these guidelines is Problem Solving, Reasoning and Numeracy. The EYFS runs from birth to the end of the child's year in school in which they reach their fifth birthday and the guidelines suggest Early Learning Goals which most children will have achieved by then.

Using numbers as labels and for counting

Before children can learn to count, they will need to become familiar with number names and show an interest in numbers. The three-year-old will typically begin to show a curiosity about numbers and to use some number names in spontaneous play. They will enjoy joining in with number rhymes and songs and begin to use mathematical language in their play such as 'lots' or 'two please'. Older pre-school children tend to offer comments about numbers or ask questions about them, perhaps making attempts to count out and to recognise numbers. They begin to develop one-to-one correspondence and are able to count out three or four objects by saying one number for each object counted out. They begin to be able to count objects not only when they are arranged in a line but also when they are scattered randomly, because their visual memories have become stronger too. By the end of the reception year, most four and five-year-olds can count up to ten objects reliably, recognise numerals from 1 to 9 and use some of their mathematical ideas to solve practical problems.

Learning how to calculate

The first step towards learning how to calculate will be the ability to compare two sets of objects and decide whether they have the same number. Three-year-olds typically begin to show an interest in number problems such as who has more or whether two of them have the same. They learn through their play that they can separate and divide up a group of objects in different ways but that the total number remains the same. The birth of adding and subtracting comes when they learn to find the total number of two groups by counting and that they can take objects away and end up with *less*. The more they handle quantity, play with quantity and count quantity, the more familiar and confident they become in calculating *how many*. They soon reach the stage where they can predict *one more than* or *one less than* a given number. By the time they reach the end of the EYFS, most children will be using the vocabulary involved in simple addition and subtraction such as 'I had two and I gave one away so I have one left.' They will use language such as *more* and *less* to compare two quantities and be more confident about combining two groups in order to *add* and taking away objects to *subtract*.

Understanding shapes, spaces and measures

Measurement involves an understanding of how things compare and change and tends to develop from an earlier understanding of spaces, shapes and sequences. Many activities to encourage this have been introduced in the first three chapters. Most pre-school children will have started to use positional language such as *there* and *under*. They will also be using *size* language in their play such as *big* and *small*. This early language and understanding will develop as they become interested in construction toys and modeling materials. Gradually, the four-year-old builds up concentration when playing with construction toys and begins to be able to plan ahead which involves an understanding of how the spaces and shapes he is dealing with are going to fit together.

With puzzles and shape inset boards comes the ability to work out that shapes occupy different kinds of spaces when they are rotated or turned over. With this comes an understanding of symmetry and orientation. He becomes able to select and cut materials to fit a given size and shape and to begin to select on the basis of length or thickness.

By the time he has reached the end of the EYFS, he will probably be using language such as *bigger*, *smaller*, *longer* and *shorter*. He will be able to talk about, recreate and copy simple patterns and he will be using simple language to describe this such as *round* or *flat*. He will be using everyday words to describe position and be beginning to use his mathematical ideas and methods to solve practical problems, such as how to design a bridge that stands or how to model something that will roll down a slope.

Supporting their learning

- Keep using number language whenever you can and in many different situations.

- Provide plenty of numerals for children to handle in different materials and textures.

- Use giant dice and play games in which you count the spots and take giant steps.

- Count steps and objects as often as you can, starting with numbers to five and then building up to ten.

- Display numbers in your setting or home – how many cups go on the shelf, or how many aprons on the hooks.

- Use *missing number* problems to make them think – for example if one number card is missing from a pack.

- Make a number line by hanging number cards from a line across the ceiling.

- Peg up socks and put in one, two or three objects to be felt for and counted.

- Use a feely bag for children to feel and identify quantity.

- Use circle time to develop confidence in early number skills. You will find a chapter full of ideas and activities for doing this in *Learning through Play: Circle Time* (Mortimer, 1998).

- Challenge children to 'find a shape like this' in their surroundings and talk about it.

- Talk about the past and the future so that children begin to develop a sense of time.

- Use picture or photograph sequences to show a child what will be happening that day or in the coming weeks.

- Use sand and water play to develop language of quantity and change such as *empty* and *more*. Always pair the word with the concrete experience.

- Use imaginative and role play to help the children develop an understanding of quantity and of how to organise spaces and shapes such as making Teddy's bed or laying a table for tea.

- Play 'peek-a-boo' games by just revealing a corner of an object or shape – can the children work out what the shape looks like?

- Cut up cards and packaging to make simple jigsaws. Start with just one or two straight cuts and then move on to curved cuts. Can the children match the pieces together?

- Pretend to be a robot and ask the children to give you directions about where to go next.

- You will find many more activities for developing children's skills and learning in the early years in the Learning and Development Grids of the *EYFS Practice Guidance* (DfES, 2007).

Chapter Five

Supporting children with special educational needs

In this chapter, we consider how to include those children who have special educational needs (SEN) in the area of mathematical development and how you can plan, along with the child, parents and carers, how to support their learning.

Perhaps a child is having more difficulty in problem solving, reasoning and numeracy than most children her age, despite all your usual approaches and opportunities. In other words, perhaps that child seems to need *additional* and *different* ways of teaching if she is to make progress. If this is the case, then this is another way of saying that the child has special educational needs (or 'SEN') as far as mathematical development is concerned. You may know the reason (perhaps she has been born with a learning disability or perhaps she has had problems with her vision) or you may not (perhaps she is developing more slowly than others for a variety of reasons). What you *can* explore is what she is able to do and what sort of help seems to work best.

Writing 'SMART' targets for problem solving, reasoning and numeracy

If you decide that a child has SEN, then you share this with parents and plan together how you can help and support the child's learning. The *SEN Code of Practice* (DfES, 2001) tells you how you should do this. In it, we are advised to write Individual Education Plans (IEPs) for children with SEN containing three or four key teaching targets. The suggestion is that the targets should be SMART – Specific (written in terms of what the child will actually do at the end of the intervention), Measurable, Achievable (so that the child can experience success despite their SEN), Relevant (to the EYFS framework) and Time-bound (usually within a term). The targets that you list should be clear to everyone who reads them. Some statements are vague and give you no clear idea of what the child is doing at the time and what they *will* be doing when the target is achieved.

Examples of vague statements are:

- 'Jodie will understand number better.' How will you know when Jodie will have achieved this?

- 'Luke's mathematical skills will be more age-appropriate.' What does this actually mean?

Instead, aim for targets that are clear and measurable:

- 'Jodie will join in with counting rhymes, counting out loud to three.'

- 'Jodie will complete a four-piece jigsaw puzzle.'

- 'Luke will be able to make two sets of objects the same number up to five.'

- 'Luke will find "one more than" a given number of counters up to three.'

Case study

Jodie has concentration and learning difficulties and finds it hard to concentrate for any length of time. As a first step, her playleaders felt that it would be appropriate to teach her to hold her concentration for a few minutes with an adult close by to encourage her. This fits well with one of the term's targets on her Individual Education Plan which states:

'Jodie will complete a four-piece jigsaw puzzle.'

They have considered the stepping stone that they would like to teach towards, since the actual early learning goals are still too difficult for Jodie to achieve, and they have used the *EYFS Practice Guidance* (DfES, 2007) for ideas. Having decided on an area to work on, that of shape awareness, they have selected an IEP target which they feel will be successful. The staff realise that they cannot teach this straight away, and so they have used *differentiation* to break the steps down into six easier stages. They did this by using a process called *task analysis*, breaking the steps down step by small step. You can see an example of this below. They have gradually built up the choices Jodie must think about; they have taught the various skills that make up the final step (such as being able to fit the pieces together); and they have gradually reduced the amount of help she is receiving. They have also been clear about the resources they will use and the support she will receive, doing their best to include Jodie's learning with the other children in the group. Finally, they have built in some follow-up at home, involving parents' help too.

Step-by-Step Planning Sheet

Name: *Jodie.*

Nature of difficulty: *Concentration.*

Area of Learning: *Problem Solving, Reasoning and Numeracy.*

IEP target:

Jodie will complete the four-piece jigsaw puzzle of the giraffe – with a helper sitting beside her to support and encourage her.

Steps along the way	**Date achieved**
1) *Jodie will place the last piece in the jigsaw when her helper has placed all the other pieces into position and then uses hand-over-hand.*	*16/05/08*
2) *Jodie will place the last piece in the jigsaw when her helper has placed all the other pieces into position and then points.*	*23/05/08*

---

3)   Jodie will do this without her helper pointing.   02/06/08

*4)   Jodie will place the last two pieces into
      the jigsaw when the other pieces have been
      placed for her.*

*5)   Jodie will complete the puzzle if her helper
      prompts her with pointing.*

*6)   Jodie will complete the puzzle independently,
      with her helper encouraging her.*

Resources and support needed:

The giraffe four-piece jigsaw in Blue Room cupboard.

*Dave will be Jodie's helper for this activity, working in a small
group of four children.*

Help from parents:

*Mr and Mrs Brown will play with shape-form boards at home
with Jodie. We will lend them these to take home.*

Activities to support SEN

Children with learning difficulties need their learning experiences to be concrete and practical so we need to think about how to make the learning steps small and the activities as motivating as possible. Here are a few suggestions.

Put it in a sock!
This activity helps children to say and use numbers in order in familiar contexts.

You need three colourful adult-sized socks, a low washing line, some pegs and six small teddy bears. Hang the washing line up at one end of your room so that it is within child's height, but lies just in front of a wall so that children do not bump into it. Peg the three socks in a row. Challenge the children to place one teddy in the first, two teddies into the second, and three teddies into the third. Have the teddies' heads peeping out the top if you can. Now get them to cover their eyes as you rearrange the socks. Can they see how many teddies are in each sock? Now tuck the teddies deep into the socks and rearrange the order. Can they *feel* this time how many are in each sock? Support them as they re-hang the socks in order, from left to right along the line.

Hide and seek
This game helps children to use everyday words to describe position.

You need a big and a little teddy bear, a toy bed with bedclothes and a small box, large enough to put the little teddy in. Gather everyone together, sitting in a circle on the floor. Introduce Little Ted to the children and show off her beautiful bed and bedclothes and her 'toy box'. Show her playing in her bedroom and then becoming tired. 'Here comes Mummy Ted to put her to bed, but oh dear! Teddy is hiding!'

Turn to the first child in the circle and ask him or her to hide Little Ted 'in the box' or 'under the bed'. Make Mummy Ted look for Little Ted and ask the children to help her by telling her where Little Ted is hiding; 'She's *in* the box!' 'She's *under* the bed!'

Develop the story as each child has a turn following your instructions and hiding Little Ted in a different place. Sing a 'goodnight' song to Little Ted together.

Countdown challenge
This activity helps children to say and use number names in order.

You need a hoop and ten coloured beanbags (or other objects that are easy to count). You also need a set of ten cards, each with the numeral 1 to 10 written on it, and a football rattle or party whistle. Gather the children on the floor, sitting in a circle. Tell them that you are going to play a counting game. Place the hoop on the floor in the middle of the circle. Arrange three number cards for 1, 2 and 3 on the floor, numeral side up. Start with one of the older children. Place three beanbags in the circle and invite them to find the correct number card and place it in the circle with the beanbags. Cheer their success and wave your rattle. Give each child a turn and gradually increase the numbers in the sets and the range of number cards you are matching. You will be able to choose a task at the right level of ability for each child.

More please!
This helps children to begin to use the vocabulary involved in adding and subtracting in practical activities and discussion.

You need your usual home corner with kitchen equipment, cups, saucers, play food, dolls, beds, table, chairs, etc. Start by playing with the child whom you are targeting and one other child in the home corner. Suggest that the first child makes tea for you all. Help them to put out plates, one for each person in the house. 'Do we need *more*?' Use pointing to show the child who will have each plate so that you can help them work out how many are needed. Do the same thing with the chairs round the table and with the saucers. Then help them to work out how many cups are needed for the saucers. Again, emphasise the key word '*more*'. Share the food onto the plates, and encourage the child whom you are targeting to ask whether the children want *more*. Keep the flow of the game as informal as possible, looking for natural opportunities to encourage the child to both respond to and use the word *more*. As more children join the game, look for *more* chairs, plates, cups, etc.

One more step
This game helps children to count one, two or three steps.

You need a series of paving stones or floor tiles which are one child's stride between each other. Number three consecutive squares 1, 2 and 3 with chalk. Gather the children in a row, all holding hands with you. Tell them that you are going to play a counting game. Can they see the numbers? Face the first tile and chant '1, 2, 3' as you take three strides together from tile to tile. Now help them balance as you have fun taking three strides backwards, counting '3, 2, 1'. Ask parents to support early counting at home by counting stairs together each time they go up or down with their child.

Children with autistic spectrum disorders

Children who have difficulties within the autistic spectrum are often very good at working with puzzles and solving *non-verbal* problems where words are not involved. Sometimes they will be so interested in numbers that they will be able to notice and identify them long before other children their age. If you are working in a group, you can choose number and puzzle activities for all the children as a way of including everyone. Here are some ideas.

Puzzle time
This game helps all the children to recognise and recreate simple patterns and allows individual children to show off a particular strength in puzzle matching.

Put out a selection of jigsaw puzzles and inset boards, both for table top and floor. Include different levels of difficulty. You might plan a 'sponsored puzzle day' as a way of fund-raising. If you ask for sponsorship for the number of puzzles completed by the group as a whole and not by individual children, then the competitive aspect is removed. Ask one helper to keep a count of each puzzle completed and cheer each completion. If necessary, you can help children by pointing to pieces to be fitted in next.

Number lotto
This game helps children to recognise numerals 1 to 9.

You will need a set of plastic numerals 1 to 9 (or draw some on cards) and a sheet of card marked into a 3 x 3 grid, with one of the numbers written into each square of the grid. Sit down with the child at a table. Support the child as he chooses one number at a time, names it and matches that number to the similar one on their sheet of card. Continue until all the numbers are placed in their correct positions.

Number spotting
This activity will help children to identify numbers on everyday notices and packaging.

Have ready some small cards and a pen. Write a large number (from 1 to 9) on a card. Invite the child to carry the card and go on a hunt with you around the setting or the home to find another number just the same. Refer the child back to the number you have drawn to compare whether the two numbers are the same. Continue with other numbers. Explore packaging, calendars, magazines or your wall posters to see if you can find numbers that are the same as the one on your card.

1 – 2 – 3 – GO!
This game encourages the first words in a child whose language or communication skills might be delayed. It is based on listening, waiting and action.

It can be very difficult for a child with communication difficulties to appreciate that he or she must wait for your word before doing something. This game makes it more fun to do so and you can play it with one child or several. Make up an imaginative game in which you become the carriages of a train, one of you behind the other(s). Encourage all your 'carriages' to 'wait on the track'. Is everyone looking? Is everyone listening? Good! Now set the children a simple challenge. 'When I say "Go" I want you all to puff to the wall' or 'When I say "Go" I want you all to drive to the engine shed' (or whatever you select). Keep your instruction simple and emphasise key words so that each child can understand. Then say '1 – 2 – 3 – GO!' Praise them for listening well and repeat with a new challenge.

Children with visual difficulties

For a child whose vision does not develop normally, the early links that most children make in co-ordinating what they feel with what they see are going to be very different. It is difficult to explore your world actively when you have no idea what is beyond your immediate surroundings. It is hard to play imaginatively with a doll's house if it feels nothing like the real thing. After all, to a sighted child, a miniature house and its contents at least looks like the real thing. If you can understand some of the differences in the way children with visual impairment learn, you will be able to plan more effective and inclusive approaches. Here are some ideas for supporting their problem solving, reasoning and numeracy.

Feeling big
This game helps children to use language such as 'bigger' and 'smaller' and to identify 'the big one' by feel.

You will need a drawstring bag with a big and small ball, big and small car, big and small brick, and big and small teddy bear – each identical to the other apart from size. Place two matching objects into the bag. Talk about them as the children watch you: 'I have a really big ball here (pause to show the children) and this one feels just the same except that it's small' (pause again to emphasise the key word). Now challenge the children in turn to put their hands into the bag and take out the big ball or the small ball. Try this for the different pairs of objects. Encourage any child with visual impairment to help you place the objects into the bag so that they can feel the big ball and the small ball in turn as you talk about their size. They will then find it easier to identify them by touch.

Sand hunt
This helps children to use everyday words to describe position and locate and identify objects by their touch.

39

You will need a sand tray or sand pit and a selection of about six small plastic animals, toys and vehicles. Ask the child or children to help you carry the toys to the sand tray and play with them for a while so that you know which toys are there. After a while, suggest that the children bury all the toys in the sand. Tell them that you are going to search for them. Encourage them to watch and guess as you identify something beneath the sand. 'It's small, it's got wheels on, it's the ... (car).' Finally, set the children a challenge to do together. 'Find me all the cars.' 'Find me the large dinosaur' etc.

Clapping echo

If a child is severely visually impaired, teach them to develop a sense of echo near to hard surfaces. This is a helpful way of learning where you are in space even when you cannot see clearly. A blind child will have subconsciously been using echolocation since babyhood, but unless you consciously talk and think about it, the skill will not develop fully. In fact, many blind children make their own little noises as they move to help this skill. For this game, move into your space and stand in a circle. Call out loudly using a sing-song 'ec-ho!' (if you can imitate the two notes of the 'cuc-koo' you will have the right notes). Tell the child or children that you are going to play an echo game. You will give each child a number of claps and they can 'echo' them back to you. Stand in front of each child in turn, clapping your hands as you count anywhere from one to ten, depending on each child's ability. Encourage by counting with the child if necessary as they repeat the claps back to you. Move to another child now, crossing the circle so that your movements are not predictable. Finish by moving around the space clapping your hands and listening to how the sounds change as you approach hard surfaces.

Feely numbers

Children with any kind of sensory difficulty need to learn how numbers feel as well as how they look, how many they represent and what word we use for them. If one of the senses is weak, then we have to use multi-sensory approaches to make sure the child has as many clues as possible when working out numbers.

Make a number line using numerals cut from sandpaper and stuck onto a card. In this way, the children can feel the numbers as well as name them. Try making a set of cards with a feely number one side and a set of sandpaper or textured objects on the other – one circle or two squares, etc. Talk about numerals and count the sets together as a child with visual impairment feels for the number shape.

Children with physical difficulties

If a child has difficulty in making or co-ordinating their hands and fingers or their movement and balance, there is a risk that their whole early learning is going to be affected. For example, if they cannot move towards their worlds and rehearse the range of actions that children usually perform in order to find out about objects and toys, then their opportunities for exploration and learning will be limited. It becomes our role to understand the child's difficulties in detail and to plan ways of making sure the child has access to early learning or, as a last resort, bring the early learning to them. Here are some ideas to get you going.

Towering high

This game helps children to use developing mathematical ideas to solve a practical problem and to use words such as 'bigger' and 'smaller' to describe solid shapes. It is also a helpful way of encouraging children with physical difficulties to stack and build.

Sometimes children with physical and co-ordination difficulties are denied the opportunity to develop the control needed in placing and stacking a tower because the materials we offer them are too small. Here is an opportunity for them to learn about building towers and develop the language of size with large building materials.

You need a set of four empty boxes or cartons in different sizes, wrapping paper, scissors and sticky tape. Cut the sheets of wrapping paper into four sizes, with the largest big enough to wrap the largest box, and the smallest sheet just right for the smallest box.

Help the child to arrange the boxes and sheets of wrap in order from smallest to largest and then have fun together wrapping and sticking the presents. When your boxes are wrapped, challenge the child to stack the boxes with the largest at the bottom and the smallest at the top.

Five in a bed
In this game, children can learn to say and use number names in order and can also practise rolling over if this is an area that needs working on.

You need a group of five children. Spread a bedspread or duvet onto a carpeted floor. Invite the children to take their shoes off and lie down, all five of them, side by side along the length of it. Introduce the familiar rhyme: 'There were five in the bed and the little one said, "Roll over! Roll over!" So they all rolled over and one fell out. There were four in the bed and the little one said, …' etc.

When you get to the first of the 'roll over's, encourage all the children to roll over in the same direction and help the child at the end as they 'fall off' the bed and sit to one side. Continue the song until there is only 'one in the bed'. You can then build the number up again by singing: 'Roll back, Roll back... So they all rolled back and one got in …' Encourage everyone to roll in the opposite direction this time and add one child to the duvet each verse until you have all five back in your bed.

You can also make 'five in a bed' out of an empty shoe box. Make a material cover into which to pop five little people made from pegs.

Knocked for six
In this game, children practise counting up to six objects. It also involves developing the co-ordination to roll a ball and knock over a skittle.

You need a set of plastic skittles and a large foam ball. Start by teaching the child or children how to roll and aim a ball. Sit them down opposite one another in an open floor space and show them how to roll the large foam ball between them. If you are suitably dressed, sitting with legs splayed is a helpful way of ensuring the ball is funneled in the right direction. When they are all rolling the ball with approximate aim, set up three of the skittles about three metres away. Take it in turns to roll the ball towards the skittles until you have knocked all three over (this stops the game becoming competitive as you are working as a team). Count the skittles as they fall. How many more do we need to knock over? Build up the number of skittles to six, adding one more each time.

Specific learning difficulties

This is an umbrella term used to describe the special educational needs of children who seem to have difficulties in certain areas of their learning despite being otherwise able. There are many kinds of specific learning difficulty and one of the more unusual kinds is *dyscalculia*, a specific problem with the acquisition of numeracy. It would not make sense to give a child this kind of label in the early years since *all* children are in the process of acquiring numeracy at this stage. It makes more sense to recognise where a child's area of difficulty might be and take steps to help them learn and improve their understanding. By 'thinking developmentally' – that is, understanding how children change and develop in their understanding and skills – you can support a child by 'starting where they are at' and moving them forward step by step. *Working with Children with Specific Learning Difficulties* (Smith, 2001) provides useful starting points for children experiencing a whole range of specific learning difficulties in their early years.

Conclusion

This book has set out the various developmental stages in problem solving, reasoning and numeracy and it is hoped that this will help you make sure that all the foundations for later learning, success and confidence are laid down. Once you understand the stages that children go through, it becomes possible to break steps down so that each and every one of the children you live or work with can experience some kind of success and confidence. By getting to know children as individuals, you can identify the different pathways that their development sometimes takes.

References

DfES (2001) *The Special Educational Needs Code of Practice*. Nottingham: DfES Publications.

DfES (2007) *The Early Years Foundation Stage: Practice Guidance*. Nottingham: DfES Publications.

Mortimer, H. (1998) *Learning through Play: Circle Time*. Leamington Spa: Scholastic.

Smith, D. (2001) *Working with Children with Specific Learning Difficulties in the Early Years*. Stafford: QEd Publications.

Useful resources

El-Naggar, O. (1995) *Investigations and Problem Solving*. Stafford: QEd Publications.

Ewing, L. & Ward, I. (2001) *Word Problems: The Language of Mathematics*. Stafford: QEd Publications.

Mortimer, H. (2002) *The SEN Code of Practice in Early Years Settings*. Stafford: QEd Publications.

Mortimer, H. (2003) *100 Number Games for ages 0 to 3*. Leamington Spa: Scholastic.

Tavener, J. (2003) *100 Number Games for ages 3 to 5*. Leamington Spa: Scholastic.